EXPLORING COUNTRIES

Croatia

by Emily Rose Oachs

BLASTOFF! READERS
5

BELLWETHER MEDIA · MINNEAPOLIS, MN

Note to Librarians, Teachers, and Parents:

Blastoff! Readers are carefully developed by literacy experts and combine standards-based content with developmentally appropriate text.

Level 1 provides the most support through repetition of high-frequency words, light text, predictable sentence patterns, and strong visual support.

Level 2 offers early readers a bit more challenge through varied simple sentences, increased text load, and less repetition of high-frequency words.

Level 3 advances early-fluent readers toward fluency through increased text and concept load, less reliance on visuals, longer sentences, and more literary language.

Level 4 builds reading stamina by providing more text per page, increased use of punctuation, greater variation in sentence patterns, and increasingly challenging vocabulary.

Level 5 encourages children to move from "learning to read" to "reading to learn" by providing even more text, varied writing styles, and less familiar topics.

Whichever book is right for your reader, Blastoff! Readers are the perfect books to build confidence and encourage a love of reading that will last a lifetime!

This edition first published in 2017 by Bellwether Media, Inc.

No part of this publication may be reproduced in whole or in part without written permission of the publisher. For information regarding permission, write to Bellwether Media, Inc., Attention: Permissions Department, 5357 Penn Avenue South, Minneapolis, MN 55419.

Library of Congress Cataloging-in-Publication Data

Names: Oachs, Emily Rose.
Title: Croatia / by Emily Rose Oachs.
Description: Minneapolis, MN : Bellwether Media, Inc., 2017. | Series:
   Blastoff! Readers: Exploring Countries | Includes bibliographical
   references and index.
Identifiers: LCCN 2015049299 | ISBN 9781626174030 (hardcover : alkaline paper)
Subjects: LCSH: Croatia–Juvenile literature.
Classification: LCC DR1510 .O23 2017 | DDC 949.72–dc23
LC record available at http://lccn.loc.gov/2015049299

Library of Congress Cataloging-in-Publication Data

Text copyright © 2017 by Bellwether Media, Inc. BLASTOFF! READERS and associated logos are trademarks and/or registered trademarks of Bellwether Media, Inc. SCHOLASTIC, CHILDREN'S PRESS, and associated logos are trademarks and/or registered trademarks of Scholastic Inc.

Printed in the United States of America, North Mankato, MN.

Contents

Croatia is a small arc-shaped country in southeastern Europe's Balkan **Peninsula**. It spans only 21,851 square miles (56,594 square kilometers). In the north sits Zagreb, Croatia's capital and largest city. The waters of the Adriatic Sea lie to the country's west. More than 1,100 small islands dot the sea near the long coast.

Croatia curves around Bosnia and Herzegovina. It forms the country's western and northern boundaries. Croatia's southernmost tip shares its border with Montenegro. The two countries touch for about 12 miles (19 kilometers). Serbia is Croatia's northeastern neighbor. Hungary and Slovenia line Croatia's northern border.

Did you know?
Croatia and its neighbors once formed a country called Yugoslavia. In 1991, Croatia became an independent country.

Hungary

Slovenia

Serbia

Zagreb

Croatia

Bosnia and Herzegovina

Adriatic Sea

Montenegro

! fun fact
Nikola Tesla was a famous inventor born in the mountains of today's Croatia. Tesla was the first to capture the power of North America's Niagara Falls. He turned it into electricity!

Dinaric Alps

The rugged Dinaric Alps trail through central Croatia from northwest to southeast. Thick forests blanket their lower slopes. This mountain range divides Croatia into two parts. To the northeast are the flat Pannonian **Plains**. They stretch across eastern Croatia and into Hungary and Serbia.

The Istrian peninsula and the Dalmatia region lie west of the mountains. Their Adriatic coasts are famous for beautiful beaches, bays, and coves. Along the sea, winters are rainy. Summers are warm and dry. Farther from the coast, winters are cold but summers have warm temperatures.

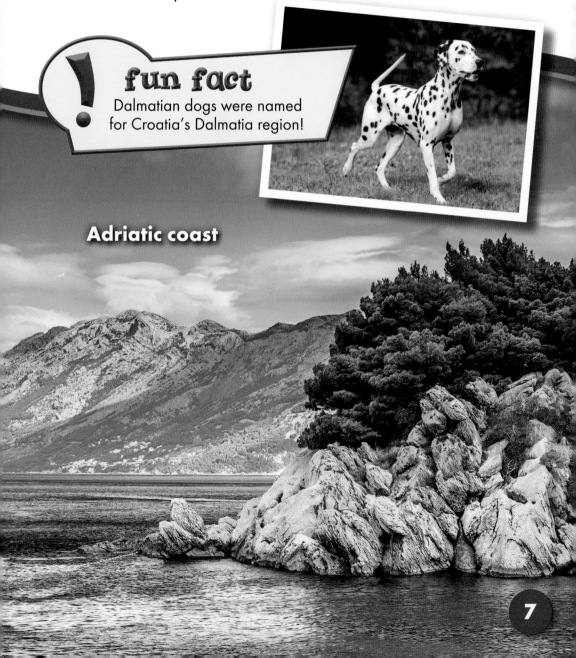

fun fact

Dalmatian dogs were named for Croatia's Dalmatia region!

Adriatic coast

Plitvice Lakes National Park

Did you know?

In 1949, the Plitvice Lakes became a national park. Today, millions of people visit to see the park's natural beauty and wildlife.

8

The Plitvice Lakes sit amid a vast forest in the Dinaric Alps. They are a chain of sixteen lakes filled with clear, blue-green water. Stunning waterfalls and **cascades** connect each lake to the next. A forest of beech, fir, and spruce trees surrounds them.

The lakes as they are today took thousands of years to form. **Minerals** in the water built up on the moss and bacteria that clung to underwater rocks. Over time, they formed natural dams. This created the unique scenery of the Plitvice Lakes.

coral reef

Croatia has among the widest variety of wildlife in Europe. In the mountain forests, powerful lynx hunt for wild sheep, hares, and deer. Wolves and wildcats hide between the trees. Brown bears search for food. At night, long-fingered bats flit through the dark sky. Owls, woodpeckers, and golden eagles perch in forest treetops.

lynx

leopard snake

olm

fun fact

The olm is a 1-foot (30-centimeter) long salamander. The cave-dweller never sees daylight. It can go ten years without eating!

Leopard snakes sun themselves in coastal olive groves. Spoonbills, herons, and white storks are found in Croatia's wetlands. In the Adriatic Sea, **coral reefs** hide beneath the waves. Bottlenose dolphins leap and play in the water. Sometimes rare monk seals are spotted.

Did you know?
The Croatian and Serbian languages sound very similar. But Croatian uses the Latin alphabet, while Serbian uses the Cyrillic.

More than 4 million people call Croatia home. About nine out of ten are **native** to the area. They are called Croats. Serbs are the country's largest **minority**. Their **ancestors** originally came from Croatia's neighbor, Serbia. Some Bosnians, Italians, Hungarians, and other Europeans also live within Croatia's borders.

In Croatia, religions and **ethnic** groups are closely linked. Most Croats practice Roman Catholicism. It is the country's most common religion. Serbs are often Eastern Orthodox. Most of Croatia's Bosnians are Muslim. The country's official language is Croatian. People in major cities often speak English or German as well.

Speak Croatian!

English	Croatian	How to say it
hello	bok	BOHK
good-bye	doviđenja	doh-vee-JEH-nyah
yes	da	DAH
no	ne	NEH
please	molim	MOH-leem
thank you	hvala	HVAH-lah
friend (male)	prijatelj	PREE-yah-tell
friend (female)	prijateljica	PREE-yah-TELL-heet-sa

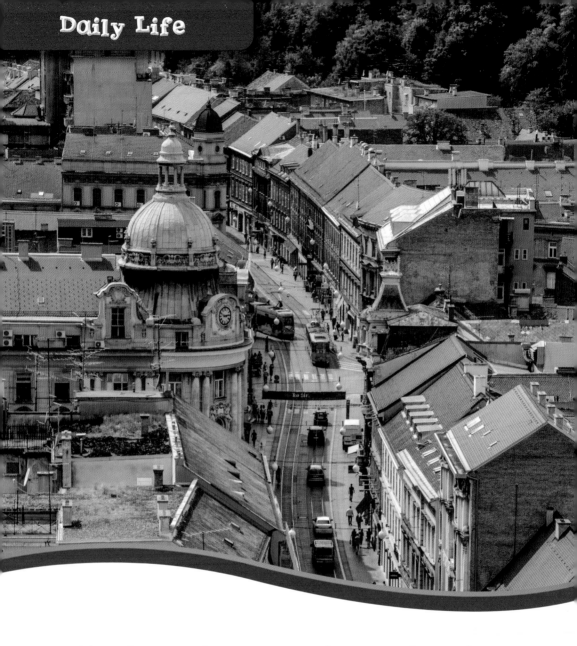

Most Croatians live in cities and towns in the northeast and near the coast. **Urban** Croatians often dwell in small apartments or houses and use buses and trams to get from place to place. They enjoy inviting friends and coworkers to their homes. Guests bring gifts of candy or flowers for their hosts.

Far fewer people live in mountain villages and other **rural** areas. There, most homes are made of stone or brick. On the coast, public ferries carry people between the islands and shore. Croatians living on Adriatic islands frequently own small boats of their own.

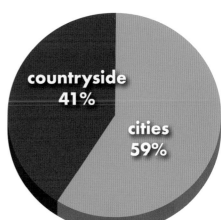

Where People Live in Croatia

countryside 41%

cities 59%

fun fact

Croats invented the first neckties, called *cravats*, in the seventeenth century. They tied fabric around their necks for their military uniforms.

15

Croatian children must attend primary school from ages 6 to 14. Most students learn to read and write in Croatian. However, the government allows minorities to be educated in their native language. This means Croatian Serbs can learn to read and write the Serbian language.

Primary school students also learn math, science, music, and another language, often English. After eight years, students can continue on to secondary school. There, they may prepare for a specific job or study the arts. Some continue general studies. After graduation, many students find jobs. Others enter one of Croatia's many universities.

fun fact

Croatia's oldest university, the University of Zagreb, was founded in 1669.

Where People Work in Croatia

services 70.4%

manufacturing 27.6%

farming 2.0%

Most Croatians hold **service jobs**. Many work in shops, schools, and offices. Others have jobs working with Croatia's **tourists**. More than 10 million people visit the country each year. They come to relax on beautiful beaches and learn about Croatia's history. Croatians serve them at local **resorts** and attractions.

The land in the Pannonian Plains is very **fertile**. There, farmers grow corn, potatoes, soybeans, and wheat. In the mountains, farmers raise sheep and cattle in pastures. Some Croatians work in factories. They make ships, chemicals, and food products. They also process the oil and natural gas that is mined from the earth.

hiking

Croatia provides many opportunities for people to enjoy the outdoors. Its national parks and protected areas attract hikers, bird watchers, and other nature lovers. In the summer, warm beaches draw crowds that sunbathe and swim. During the winter, skiers head to snowy mountain slopes. Croatians are particularly passionate about soccer. Basketball, water polo, and handball also appeal to young and old alike.

Local festivals allow people to celebrate Croatia's folk culture. Croats dress in their **traditional** clothing. Some gather in circles to perform the fast-paced *kolo* dance. Others play the stringed *tamburitza* instrument.

kolo **dance**

Near the sea, Croatians dine on fresh squid or octopus. They eat fish with a traditional dish of **Swiss chard** and potatoes, called *blitva*. Away from the coast, lamb, beef, pork, and chicken are common meats. A variety of meats goes into *cobanac*, a thick stew made in the northeast.

A favorite dish is *cevapcici*, or spiced rolls of ground meat. A cheese pastry called *gibanica* is also popular. In Croatia, lunch tends to be the largest meal of the day. Croatians may enjoy breaded **veal** with dumplings and pickles. Dinner is usually a cold meal of cheese, meat, and bread.

fun fact

Northern Croatia has a long history of baking heart-shaped gingerbread called *licitars*. Bakers paint these treats with colorful frosting. They decorate them with beautiful pictures and messages.

octopus

licitars

All Saints' Day

On June 25, Croatia celebrates Statehood Day. This holiday marks the day Croatia declared independence from Yugoslavia in 1991. To celebrate, Croatians wave flags, watch parades, and listen to speeches from their leaders. They also celebrate Independence Day on October 8. On this date, Croatia officially broke free from Yugoslavia.

fun fact

On November 1, Croatians observe All Saints' Day. They decorate the graves of loved ones with flowers and candles.

In January, costumed Croatians parade through northwestern villages to welcome spring. They wear sheepskins, special hats, and bells around their waists. Villagers watch them bump into each other to make the bells ring. Roman Catholic towns each have a **patron saint**. Each year, townspeople celebrate this holy person with ceremonies on a certain day.

For centuries, rural Croatian women have practiced the art of lacemaking. Their beautiful webs of lace are sold or used to decorate clothing. Lacemaking is centered in Croatia's towns of Pag, Hvar, and Lepoglava. Each produces a different type of lace.

Pag's needlepoint lace features designs of branching shapes. Hvar women weave aloe lace using delicate threads from aloe plants. For **bobbin** lace, women in Lepoglava braid and twist threads wrapped around a round bobbin. In 2011, a competition in Russia named Croatia's bobbin lace the world's most beautiful. Around the world, people celebrate Croatia's outstanding artistic traditions.

bobbin lace

Pag
lace

Fast Facts About Croatia

Croatia's Flag

The Croatian flag features horizontal red, white, and blue stripes. These colors were inspired by the colors on Russia's flag. The nation's coat of arms is at the flag's center. The coat of arms bears five smaller shields. These shields stand for the historic regions of Croatia: Croatia, Dubrovnik, Dalmatia, Istria, and Slavonia. This flag was adopted in 1990.

Official Name: Republic of Croatia

Area: 21,851 square miles (56,594 square kilometers); Croatia is the 127th largest country in the world.

Capital City:	Zagreb
Important Cities:	Split, Dubrovnik
Population:	4,464,844 (July 2015)
Official Language:	Croatian
National Holidays:	June 25 (Statehood Day); October 8 (Independence Day)
Religions:	Roman Catholic (86.3%), Orthodox Christian (4.4%), Muslim (1.5%), other (4%), none (3.8%)
Major Industries:	tourism, manufacturing, mining, agriculture
Natural Resources:	oil, clay, natural gas, salt
Manufactured Products:	chemicals, oil products, ships, steel, food products
Farm Products:	pigs, corn, wheat, poultry, potatoes, grapes, olives
Unit of Money:	kuna; the kuna is divided into 100 lipas.

Glossary

ancestors—relatives who lived long ago

bobbin—a round spool used to wind thread

cascades—small, steep waterfalls

coral reefs—structures made of coral that usually grow in shallow seawater

ethnic—related to a group of people with a specific cultural background

fertile—able to support growth

minerals—substances found naturally in the earth

minority—a group of people who are different than the largest group in an area

native—originally from a specific place

patron saint—a saint who is believed to look after a country or a group of people

peninsula—a section of land that extends out from a larger piece of land and is almost completely surrounded by water

plains—large areas of flat land

resorts—vacation spots that offer recreation, entertainment, and relaxation

rural—related to the countryside

service jobs—jobs that perform tasks for people or businesses

Swiss chard—a type of beet with large leaves that are often cooked as a vegetable

tourists—people who travel to visit another place

traditional—relating to a custom, idea, or belief handed down from one generation to the next

urban—related to cities and city life

veal—the meat of young cattle

To Learn More

AT THE LIBRARY
Brlic-Mazuranic, Ivana. *Croatian Tales of Long Ago.*
London, U.K.: Forgotten Books, 2015.

Gay, Marie-Louise, and David Homel. *The Traveling Circus.* Ontario, Can.: Groundwood Books, 2015.

Rusch, Elizabeth. *Electrical Wizard: How Nikola Tesla Lit Up the World.* Somerville, Mass.: Candlewick Press, 2013.

ON THE WEB
Learning more about Croatia is as easy as 1, 2, 3.

1. Go to www.factsurfer.com.

2. Enter "Croatia" into the search box.

3. Click the "Surf" button and you will see a list of related web sites.

With factsurfer.com, finding more information is just a click away.

Index

The images in this book are reproduced through the courtesy of: Andrei Rybachuk, front cover; Volina, pp. 4-5; Frank Fischbach, p. 6; otsphoto, p. 7 (top); Gaspar Janos, p. 7 (bottom); Creative Travel Projects, pp. 8-9; Sphinx Wang, p. 9; WaterFrame/ Alamy, pp. 10-11; Jazzer, p. 11 (top left); Matteo photos, p. 11 (top right); Nature Picture Library/ Alamy, p. 11 (bottom); Zvonimir Atletic, p. 12; pavel dudek, p. 14; xbrchx, p. 15; Xinhua/ Alamy, pp. 16-17; paul prescott, p. 18; paul prescott/ Alamy, p. 19 (left); Martin Moxter/ imagebr/ imageBROKER/ SuperStock, p. 19 (right); imageBROKER/ Alamy, pp. 20, 27; Aleksandar Todorovic, p. 21; Ladi Kirn/ Alamy, p. 22; JGA, p. 23 (left); Delimir Hrestak, p. 23 (right); Alen Gurovic/ Alamy, pp. 24-25, 26; vuk8691, pp. 26-27; Tom K Photo, p. 29.